"I am th

REMEMBER THE
Fifties
A pictorial history of an intriguing decade

Bath · New York · Singapore · Hong Kong · Cologne · Delhi
Melbourne · Amsterdam · Johannesburg · Auckland · Shenzhen

This edition published by Parragon in 2011

Parragon
Queen Street House
4 Queen Street
Bath, BA1 1HE

Created and produced by:
Endeavour London Ltd.
21-31 Woodfield Road
London W9 2BA

With great thanks to the team at Endeavour London Ltd.—Jennifer Jeffrey, Kate Pink, Franziska Payer-Crockett and Liz Ihre

Text © Parragon Books Ltd 2007

ISBN 978-1-4454-4336-2

Printed in China

All rights reserved.

DVD produced by Getty Images.

Running time of DVD is approximately 30 minutes.

All images courtesy of Getty Images who is grateful to the following photographers and image libraries represented by Getty Images for their kind assistance.

20th Century Fox: 14, 126; Agence France Presse: 99, 105-107, 109-110, 124, 146, 178, 182, 208(t), 242-243; CBS Archives: 171; Columbia Pictures: 121, 248; Daiei Studios: 16; Ernst Haas: 36; MGM: 54-55, 84, 249; Paramount Pictures: 15; Ponti-De Laurentiis Cinematografica: 120; Roger Viollet: 250; Time & Life Pictures: frontispiece, 8-13, 15, 17(b), 18-21, 24-27(b), 29, 32-33, 47, 50, 52, 62, 72, 78, 82-83, 85-86, 96-98, 100-103, 112-113, 116, 119, 121, 125, 128-129, 133, 135-137, 141, 144-145, 152-156, 160-161, 164-165, 170, 172, 174-175, 187-189, 192-193, 195, 198(t), 202-203, 207, 211, 215, 218-219, 224, 226-228, 230-237(t), 238, 240-241, 244-248, 252, 255; Ultramar Films: 17(t); United Artists: 17(b), 56, 85; Warner Brothers: 57, 149

Cover images clockwise from left to right:

Buddy Holly, 1959. © Michael Ochs Archives/Getty Images

A wide-angle lens' view of the Solomon R Guggenheim Museum, New York City, NY, 1959. © Time & Life Pictures/Getty Images

Men of the US 187th Regiment prepare to attack a ridge, Korean War 1951. © AFP/Getty Images

Evangelist Billy Graham preaching at Madison Square Garden, 1957.
© Time & Life Pictures/Getty Images

Sleeping Beauty's castle in Disneyland, California 1955.
© Time & Life Pictures/Getty Images

The United States explode their first H-Bomb, Eniwetok Atoll, Marshall Islands, 1952. © Time & Life Pictures/Getty Images

President Dwight D Eisenhower speaking to the crowd outdoors, 1953.
© Time & Life Pictures/Getty Images

The Ten Commandments shown at a drive-in movie theater, 1956.
© Time & Life Pictures/Getty Images

Marilyn Monroe in a publicity still for Gentlemen Prefer Blondes, 1953.
© Time & Life Pictures/Getty Images

Middle image:

Elvis Presley in a publicity handout for his film Love Me Tender, 1956.
© Getty Images

Frontispiece

General Douglas MacArthur roars his orders from the flagship USS Mount McKinley, as his 1st Marine Division makes its assault landing on the Inchon beach-head, Korea, September 15, 1950.

Page 7

Crowds flock to the Ford stand at the Paris Motor Show, October 22, 1956. The object of their dreams was the Firebird II, a concept car with titanium body, a gas turbine engine, and flair.

Book Contents

DVD Contents

Introduction

The 1950s formed a decade of transition between old and new worlds. The dust finally settled on the ruins of World War II. New houses emerged for the masses, West Germany was recognized as a sovereign state. Japan was re-admitted to the brotherhood of nations. Swords were made into ploughshares, or rather cars, cookers, TVs, food processors, scooters, bubble cars, and LPs. The first supermarkets opened, and junk food appeared. There was a glut of coffee shops. Cut-price *chic* filled store windows as fashion imitators copied the creations of the great dress designers.

Politically, the Fifties resolved some old problems and created a set of new ones. The Suez Crisis dealt a hammer blow to the old British Empire. War in Indo-China drove the French from Southeast Asia, and established North and South Vietnam. A young lawyer named Fidel Castro led the revolution that drove the corrupt Batista regime from Cuba and built a Communist state in America's back-yard. Like so many conflicts, the Korean War finished where it started, leaving a dispute that was still unresolved 50 years later.

Abstract art flourished, Surrealism survived, organic architecture sprouted from the ground, and—in the *argot* of the era—serial music proved to be a "killer". In the hands of Rodgers and Hammerstein, the Broadway musical turned operatic. The orchestras of Stan Kenton and Duke Ellington turned symphonic. Rock 'n' Roll raised the roof. With a whole lotta shakin' on TV and stage, and a whole lotta screamin' from the fans, the King made his debut, and *Heartbreak Hotel* became a million-seller.

Hollywood successfully fought off television's first attack, with stereoscopic sound and wide screen images. Newspapers thrived. Soccer's World Cup returned in 1950, to the delight of all Brazil. The 1952 and 1956 Olympiads blazed with glory in Helsinki and Melbourne respectively. Crowds surged to the race-track, boxing arena, and sports field. For a few more years golf remained an old-man's game, one for the wealthy and worn-out.

But the fearsome Sword of Damocles hanging over it all was the Bomb.

By 1950 the **Apartheid** system was well-established in South Africa, an economic miracle for the whites and little more than slavery for the blacks. (*Left*) Workers on a farm jail built and maintained by white farmers. The inmates received no pay.

🔘 *Track 1*

The barbed wire fence that
marked the boundary of the
Moroka township in **Soweto**,
Johannesburg. Life was
already bad for such families.
It was to get worse.

🔊 *Track 1*

A brave piece of graffiti on a plinth in the city center of **Johannesburg**, where the message "GOD IS BLACK" has been chalked. To the authorities, God was most decidedly white.

(*Above*) American film director Billy Wilder in another of **Eames's plastic chairs**. The flexibility of the thin strip metal base enabled the sitter to use it as a rocking chair.

Fifties design made much of modern techniques and modern materials, with plastic and chrome very popular. (*Left*) The American designer Charles Eames relaxes in a **moulded plastic chair** on the beach at the Pacific Palisades, California in August 1950.

The Oscar for Best Picture of
1950 went to **All About Eve**.
(*Above*, left to right) Celeste
Holm, Bette Davis, and Hugh
Marlowe fasten their seat
belts for a bumpy night.

A rival nomination for
Best Picture was **Sunset
Boulevard**, in which
Gloria Swanson (*right*)
played a warped version
of herself as a relic of
the silent movie era.

Kurosawa's **Rashomon** (*left*) introduced the Japanese cinema to western audiences almost single-handed, with a bravura performance by Toshiro Mifune. (*Above*) A still from Buñuel's **Los Olvidados**, a story of juvenile delinquents in the slums of Mexico City. (*Right*) José Ferrer in the title role of **Cyrano de Bergerac**.

(*Left*) A major work by a great master were the murals for the Chapelle du Rosaire in Vence (France), painted on tile by **Henri Matisse** and described by the poet Aragon as "so joyful that they turned the chapel into a ballroom". Matisse (*right*) was 80 when he created the work.

The boxer of the Fifties was **Sugar Ray Robinson**, world welterweight and middleweight champion, and a man of considerable charisma. (*Left*) Robinson at his training camp. (*Right*) Sugar Ray poses with his pink Cadillac in front of one of his two Harlem restaurants.

🔘 *Track 2*

(*Above*) Amphibious assault craft carry Marines towards Inchon in
the first major counter-attack of the Korean War, October 7, 1950.
Inchon was Seoul's port city. (*Right*) One of a series of photographs
by Bert Hardy showing Marines leaping ashore in the attack.

The Korean War

The United States and its allies viewed with dismay the advance of Communism in China and Korea, and on June 25, 1950 North Korean forces crossed the 38th Parallel and invaded South Korea. During a Soviet boycott, the UN Security Council authorized the use of force to counter the invasion, and on July 19 the first US Marines landed on the peninsula. UN troops followed in September.

The fighting was intense, a ferocious reproduction of World War II, though nuclear weapons were mercifully not used, despite the wishes of the commander Douglas MacArthur. At first the North Koreans, supported by the Chinese, carried all before them, capturing the South Korean capital of Seoul and forcing US and UN coalition armies into a relatively small area around Pusan in the south-east. Throughout the bitter winter of 1950–1951, the coalition steadily regained ground, at considerable cost. When peace came in the summer of 1953, the Americans had lost some 25,000 men, the South Koreans over a million. Losses on the North Korean and Chinese side were even greater.

(*Above*) During a lull in fighting near Haktong-ni, an American infantryman seeks to comfort one of his comrades whose friend has been killed. The helmeted soldier is filling in a list of casualties. (*Right*) Communist troops taken prisoner in the early days of the war are marched away in their underwear by Marines.

(*Left*) Major Carroll Cooper after going without sleep for three days and nights while fighting through the Yalu gorges, December 1950. (*Above*) Men of the US 187th Regiment prepare to attack a ridge, May 3, 1951. (*Right*) The moment of capture on the following day.

Although World War II had been over for six years, some items were still rationed in Britain—among them bread, meat, petrol, and sweets. (*Above*) Children bring back their household rations of **coal and coke** from the depot at Nine Elms, London. (*Right*) Two dissatisfied customers consider their **meat ration**.

Track 4

Ethel and Julius Rosenberg were found guilty of espionage and passing atomic secrets to the Soviets on March 30, 1951. On April 5 they were sentenced to death. (*Right*) Police mugshots of the Rosenbergs. (*Left*) The Rosenbergs embrace in a prison van after their arraignment in New York City.

🎵 *Track 5*

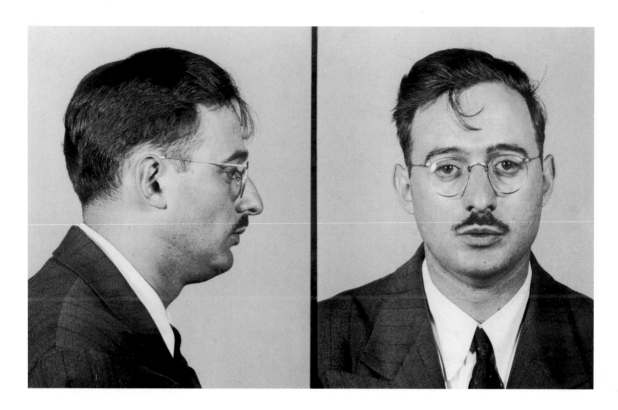

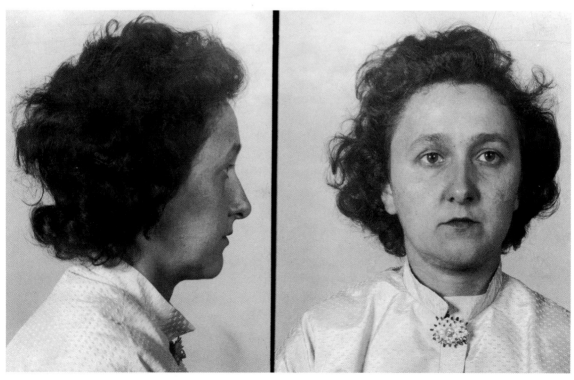

Men of power who clashed in 1951. (*Left*) **General Douglas MacArthur**, commander of the US troops in Korea and virtual plenipotentiary in the Far East, addresses a joint session of Congress, April 1951.

🔘 *Track 6*

(*Above*) President **Harry Truman** in April 1951. Appalled by MacArthur's bellicosity and threats that he would use atomic weapons, he sacked MacArthur the following month.

"All the world is coming to London, to see what we have done…" One hundred years after the Great Exhibition, London staged the **Festival of Britain** in 1951. (*Left*) Orderly queues form for entry to the Dome of Discovery, a celebration of modern science. (*Above*) The main Festival site on the South Bank, with the Festival Hall (foreground), the Dome of Discovery, and the needle-like Skylon.

As well as worthy exhibitions, the Festival provided entertainment and enjoyment for its visitors. (*Above*) A line of revelers "chassés" its way to a London **street party** during the celebrations.

There was a mammoth funfair in Battersea Park, at the heart of the Festival of Britain, with the usual swings and roundabouts and an extraordinary railway called The Far Tottering and Oystercreek Railway as well as a roller coaster, here enjoyed by two girls from the **Windmill Theatre**.

(*Above*) By some bungling bureaucratic oversight, a group of the **Ku Klux Klan** was permitted to promenade by candlelight at the Festival of Britain in the Battersea Festival Gardens on October 6. (*Right*) The Festival came to an end on November 3, 1951 with a spectacular firework display on the river, next to the Gardens.

A nightmare for the British
Secret Service was the
disappearance and
subsequent defection to the
Soviet Union of two leading
diplomats, Guy Francis de
Moncy **Burgess** (*above*)
and Donald **MacLean** (*left*).
(*Right*) As First Secretary in
the British Embassy in
Washington DC, MacLean
(far right) consults with John
Balfour, British Minister to
the United States, June 8, 1951.

The greatest racing driver of the 1950s was the Argentinian **Juan Fangio**, known as "The Maestro", five times winner of the World Championship which was inaugurated in 1950. (*Left*) Drivers line up for the start of the Reims Grand Prix on July 2, 1951. (*Right*) Fangio acknowledges the cheers of the crowd from the wheel of his Alfa Romeo after winning at Reims.

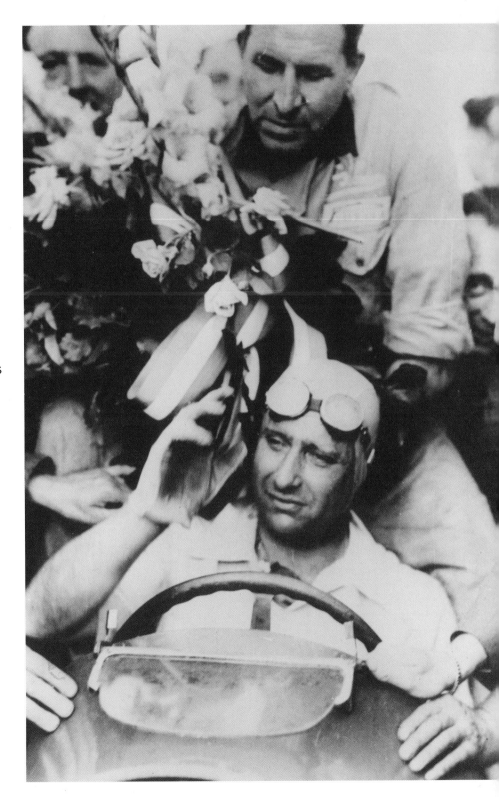

The British motor industry was slow to recover after the war, with a shortage of machine tools and a need to reconstruct most factories and production lines. (*Above*) The **Austin 7**, more usually known as the A30 or A35, was a car for the masses.

(*Above*) At the other end of the market was this **Auto-Union Porsche** convertible, here seen on display at the 36th International Motor Show at Earl's Court, London, October 16, 1951, the year of Ferdinand Porsche's death.

After being dismissed by the British electorate in 1945, **Churchill** returned to power in 1951. (*Above*) Crowds in his own Woodford constituency gather at St Barnabas School on October 26. (*Right*) The famous V-salute from the new Prime Minister.

(*Above*) A marriage that didn't last—Mohammad Reza Pahlavi, **Shah of Iran** with his bride Princess Soraya Esfandiary Bakhtiari, February 28, 1951. (*Right*) "...till death us do part..." **Margaret Hilda Roberts**—in royal-blue velvet—marries Denis Thatcher, December 13, 1951.

The world of *haute couture*... (*Left*) Three evening dresses by **Balenciaga** at a New York fashion show. The designs were inspired by the work of Toulouse-Lautrec. (*Right*) No more drawing on the leg... A model wears elaborately **seamed stockings**.

By 1951 Paris's recovery from the war and occupation was almost complete. (*Right*) An elegant *Parisienne* takes her morning aperitif in a café on the **Champs Elysées**, June 23, 1951.

(*Above*) A model poses in a yellow wool coat designed by **Alix Grès**. Madame Grès opened her first small shop on the Rue du Faubourg Saint-Honoré in the 1930s. By the 1950s she was one of the top Paris designers.

The French capital was the setting for one of MGM's lavish musicals of 1951—**An American in Paris**, which won the Oscar for Best Picture in 1951. (*Left*) Gene Kelly in the ballet "dream" sequence. (*Right*) Leslie Caron, Kelly's partner in the film.

(*Above*) Humphrey Bogart and Katharine Hepburn in the "storm-lashed" boat at Isleworth Studios, London during the making of John Huston's **The African Queen**. Bogart won an Oscar for his portrayal of Charlie Allnut. (*Right*) Marlon Brando and Vivien Leigh in the film version of **A Streetcar Named Desire**. Leigh won an Oscar for her performance as Blanche DuBois.

After the obliteration of Hiroshima and Nagasaki in 1945, the Bomb was never used again in the 20th century. Its mere existence was enough to dictate foreign policy in both East and West. Like the hottest of potatoes, the Bomb passed from Britain to the United States, and thence, via spies and traitors, to the USSR. By the 1950s, countries were queueing to obtain nuclear arsenals of their own... Israel, France, India, Pakistan... Statesmen strutting on the world stage loved the Bomb, though they habitually mentioned it in reverend tones and cautious terms. The military viewed it suspiciously, with the dishonorable exception of General MacArthur. The ordinary citizens of East and West, however, could do little but fear it.

(*Left*) **A cloud rises 3,500 feet (1,060 meters) over the Yucca Flats following one of a series of A-Bomb tests in Nevada, March 19, 1952.**

(*Above and below*) During the tests, a specially constructed house tested the effect of the atomic blast. A film camera was encased in a two-inch thick lead sheath to photograph the results. The sole illumination for the pictures was the flash from the blast itself.

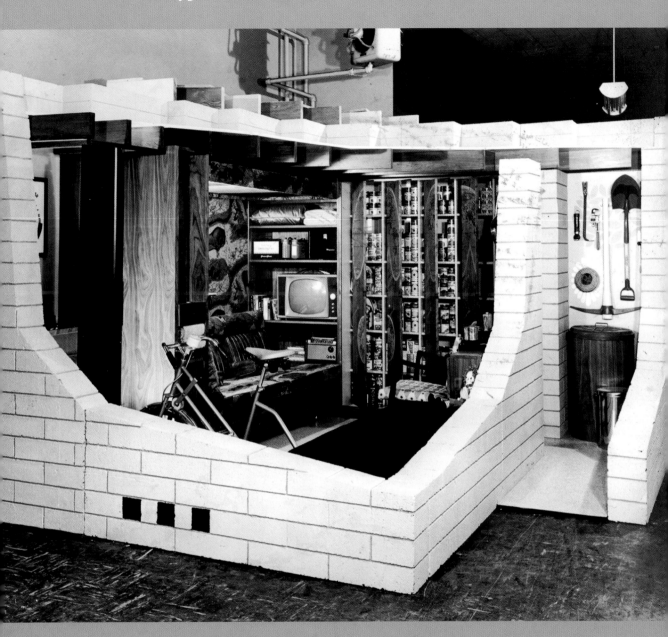

The authorities were up-beat about the chances of surviving an atomic attack. (*Left*) The fall-out shelter survival pack— all you need for the first six months following a nuclear explosion. (*Above*) The American Dream Nuclear Shelter— with pick and shovel to dig your way out.

Code name Ivy Mike... a fireball of heated gas stretches out above the Pacific after the United States explode

their first H-Bomb, Eniwetok Atoll, Marshall Islands, October 31, 1952.

While sailing from Europe to the United States, the cargo vessel **Flying Enterprise** encountered fierce storms in the North Atlantic that cracked her hull. The ship's captain, **Kurt Carlsen**, did what he could to return to Britain. Forty miles (64 kilometers) from Falmouth, the crew were lifted off when the ship's list reached 80 degrees (*left*). Carlsen (*above*) stayed on to the bitter end on January 9, 1952.

🔊 *Track 8*

🔊 *Track 9*

The British King, **George VI**, died of cancer on February 6, 1952. For several days his body lay in state in Westminster Hall (*left*), before being taken to St George's Chapel, Windsor for burial. (*Above*) The new Queen, **Elizabeth II** (right) drives with her sister Margaret from Sandringham to Westminster Hall, February 11.

In April 1952 BOAC's **Comet**, the world's first passenger jet airliner began service. Its maiden scheduled flight was from London Heathrow to Johannesburg, South Africa. A return ticket cost $630 (£315), and the 7,000-mile (11,000-kilometer) journey took 23 hours, 40 minutes. (*Above*) The Comet makes a refueling stop in Khartoum. Other stops were at Rome, Beirut, Entebbe, and Livingstone. (*Left*) Two passengers enjoy an early flight.

The **SS United States** (*above*) became the new holder of the Blue Riband for making the fastest crossing of the Atlantic—the first time an American liner held the record for 60 years. (*Right*) The *United States* arrives in Le Havre, France, after crossing in three days, 10 hours, and 40 minutes, at an average speed of 35.59 knots.

Events in Egypt moved swiftly in the summer of 1952. On July 23 **General Mohammad Naguib** (*right*) seized power, overthrowing the "playboy" **King Farouk**. Three days later, Farouk and his family left Egypt on the navy yacht *Mahroussa* (*left*) and headed for exile in Naples.

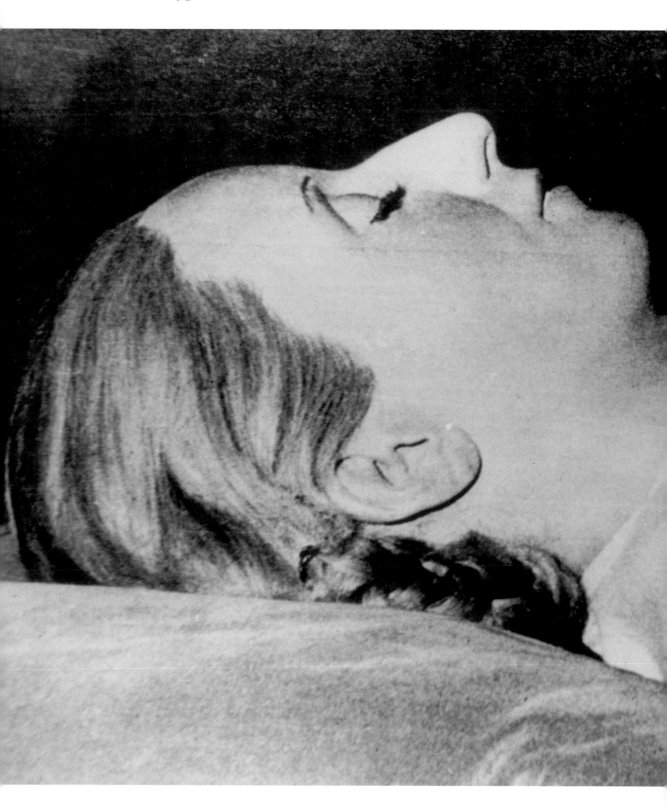

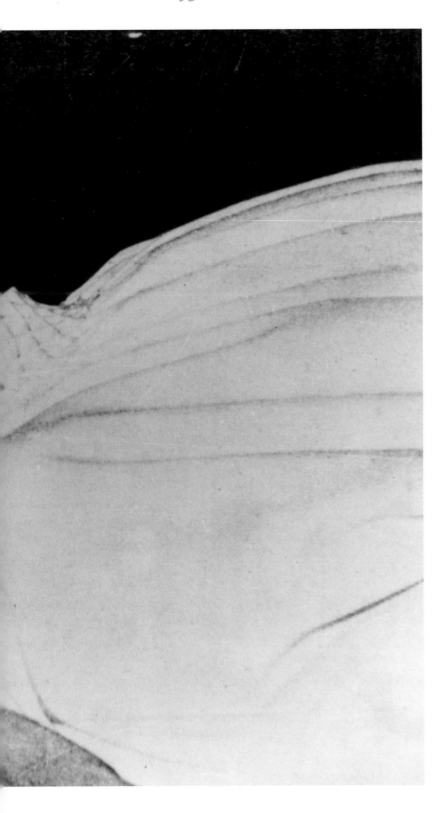

The body of **María Eva Duarte de Perón** lies in state. She died of cancer at the age of 33, mourned throughout Argentina where she had been perhaps the most influential political figure for the past six years. Certainly, as "Spiritual Leader of the Nation" in her husband's second term of office as President, she was as powerful as he was, thanks to the support given her by the Labor Unions, her own Foundation, and the Female Peronist Party.

The 1952 Olympic Games were held in Helsinki, where Germany
and Japan were once again admitted to the Olympic fold, and the United
States led the medals table with 40 Gold, 19 Silver, and 17 Bronze. (*Above*)
The star of the Games, **Emil Zatopek**, takes the lead in the 5,000 Metres
(5K), winning this event, the 10,000 Metres (10K), and the Marathon.
(*Right*) **Rusaek-Nielsen** of Denmark clears a fence ahead of his horse
in the Endurance Cross-Country Equestrian Event.

Some of the last rites of the British Empire were attended by young **national servicemen**—conscript soldiers serving their country for two fearful years. (*Left*) General Gerald Templer supervises rifle practice. (*Above*) A battle-hardened sergeant and his young platoon patrol the Malayan jungle, September 1952.

The struggle for freedom and independence in Kenya turned to violence
when the **Mau-Mau** began to attack and kill white settlers. (*Right*) A Mau-Mau
suspect is arrested by a member of the Kenyan police, November 29, 1952.
(*Above*) Mau-Mau prisoners are held in a "Special Effort Camp" near Nairobi.

In the Presidential elections **Dwight D Eisenhower** was returned to power with a landslide victory over his Democrat opponent Adlai E Stevenson. (*Above*) Stevenson campaigns in Vallejo, California in October 1952. (*Right*) "Ike" anticipates victory in Atlanta, Georgia. His Vice-Presidential running mate was Richard Nixon.

🔘 *Track 10*

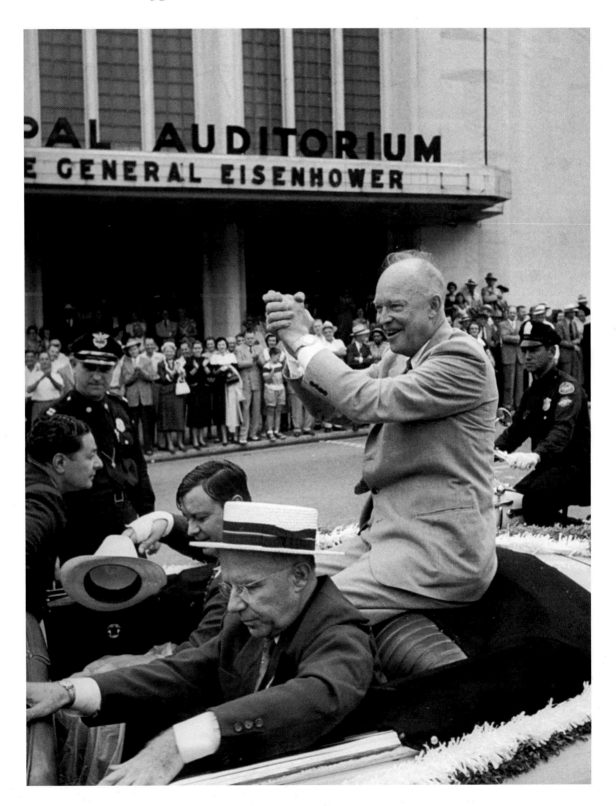

Charlie Chaplin won an Oscar in 1952 for the music score he wrote for his own film **Limelight** (*right*). Over on the MGM lot, some of the finest talent in the movie business were making the greatest musical film of all time— **Singing in the Rain**. (*Left*) Gene Kelly splashes his way through the title number.

Polio remained a scourge, a disease that struck mainly the young, condemning them to a life of paralysis, often confined to living in an **iron lung** (*left*). The great hope in the early Fifties was for cure or preventative.

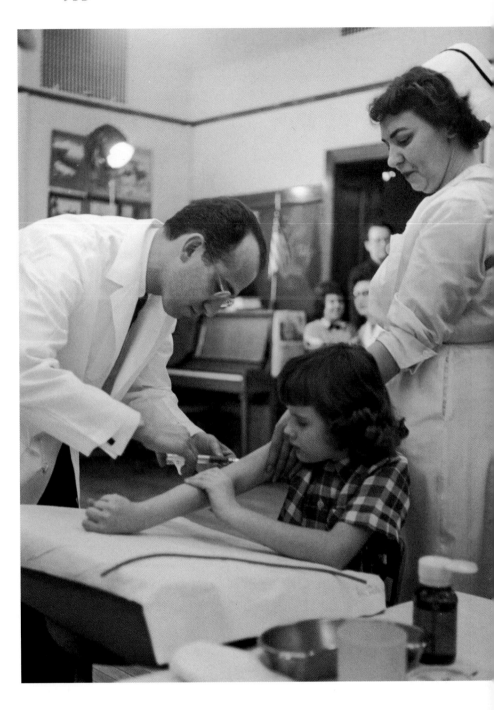

🔘 *Track 11*

The breakthrough came in 1953 with the discovery of a vaccine that could immunize entire populations from the crippling disease. (*Above*) The American **Dr Jonas Salk**, discoverer of the vaccine, treats a young girl.

(*Above*) Out with the old... **Joseph Stalin's coffin** is carried from the House of the Trade Unions, Moscow by (left to right) Shvernik, Kaganovich, Bulganin, Molotov, General Vassily Stalin, and Malenkov. Beria (far right) was executed nine months later. (*Right*) In with the new... **Queen Elizabeth II** enters Buckingham Palace after her Coronation, June 2, 1953.

🔘 *Track 12*

🔘 *Track 13*

On May 29, 1953, Sherpa Tenzing Norgay (*left*) and Edmund Hillary reached the **summit of Mount Everest**, the first men known to have done so. (*Above*—left to right) Hillary, Colonel John Hunt—leader of the expedition—and Tenzing make final adjustments to a model of Everest in preparation for a press conference at the Royal Geographical Society, July 3, 1953.

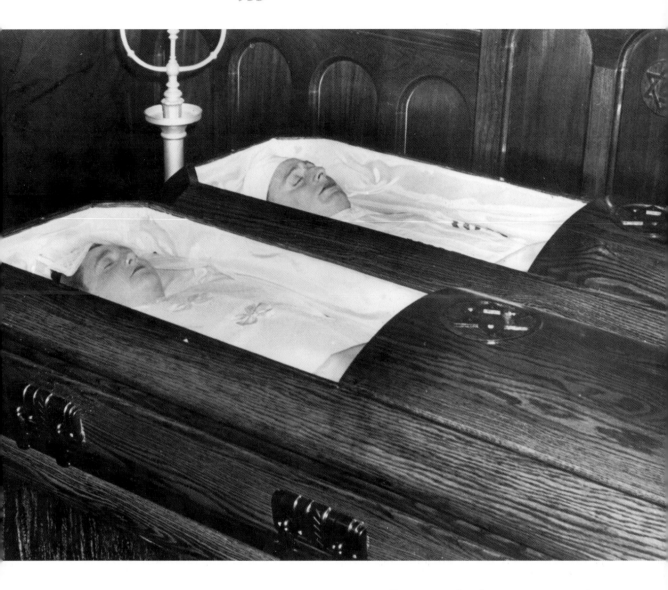

Two years after they were sentenced to death for betraying A-bomb secrets to the USSR, **Ethel and Julius Rosenberg** were executed. (*Left*) Demonstrators in Paris demand a pardon for the Rosenbergs, June 18, 1953. There was worldwide protest at the executions. (*Above*) Coffins containing the bodies of Ethel and Julius.

Violence erupted on the streets of **East Berlin** as workers demonstrated against what they considered unfair labor practices imposed by the Soviet Union. (*Above*) Columbus House burns in Potsdamer Platz, June 19, 1953. (*Left*) Young men attack a Soviet tank. (*Right*) A protest march. Over 100 people were killed during the disturbances.

The Korean War dragged on into the summer of 1953, although a programme of **POW exchanges** was implemented six months earlier. (*Left*) A Communist soldier sits with head bowed as he describes his experiences as a prisoner of UN troops. (*Above*) Newly released former POW Army Private John Ploch is processed at "Freedom Village".

Following a coup in August, **Shah Reza Pahlavi** boarded a
plane at Teheran Airport (*left*) and flew off into exile. His former
Prime Minister, **Dr Mohammed Mossadeq** was arrested by
the new regime and placed on trial. (*Above*) Mossadeq rests
his head on his lawyer's shoulder during the trial, November 11,
1953. He was sentenced to three years imprisonment.

The US "Wedding of the Year" was that of **Senator John Kennedy** to **Jacqueline Bouvier**, September 12. (*Right*) Jack and Jackie sail through their engagement.
(*Left*) Adoration and reflection at the Kennedy summer house, July 7, 1953. (*Above*) The newly married couple take their seats at the reception in Newport. Guests had to wait for their pineapple until the photo-shoot calmed down.

 Track 14

In 1947 the Adriatic port of **Trieste** had come under United Nations control. On October 19, 1953, President Tito of Yugoslavia disputed the return of part of the city to Italy. The issue became a matter of international concern, with demonstrations (*right*) and fighting between citizens (*left*) on the streets of Trieste.

A major French initiative in Indo-China was the capture of Dien Bien Phu by paratroopers under the command of **Colonel Christian de Castries**. Peace negotiations began with the Vietminh leader **Ho Chi Minh**, who predicted that the French would be defeated and replaced by US troops. (*Above*) De Castries in his underground HQ, May 23, 1954. (*Left*) Ho Chi Minh visits an orphanage in Hanoi.

On March 13, 1954, the Vietminh besieged the French stronghold of **Dien Bien Phu** in what became the fiercest battle of the war. European papers constantly reported that the French were holding their own and that reinforcements would be airlifted in, but on April 14, the Vietminh (*right*) attacked and captured the Muong Thanh airport.

Track 16

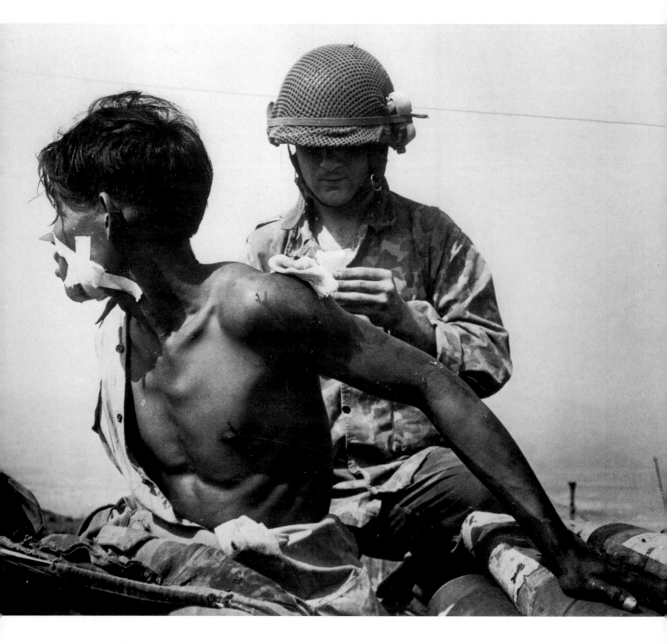

Casualties were heavy on both sides. (*Above*) **A French
military doctor** treats the wounds of a Vietminh
soldier during the last days of the siege. On May 7
the French surrendered. (*Right*) The French heroine of
the siege, Army nurse **Geneviève de Galard**, known
as "The Angel of Dien Bien Phu". She was captured by
the Vietminh but released three weeks later.

Ever since its completion in 1869, the British had held a controlling interest in the Suez Canal. The new Revolutionary Government in **Egypt** sought to put an end to that influence. (*Above*) Anti-British crowds demonstrate in Cairo, January 9, 1954. (*Left*) General Mohammad Naguib and **Colonel Gamal Abdel Nasser** (on right) leave a Revolutionary meeting, February 23, 1954.

Kenya's struggle for independence had intensified as the years passed. By 1954 the militant and murderous **Mau-Mau** were wreaking havoc among the white settlers. In retaliation, the British rounded up many Kenyans suspected of being Mau-Mau members or sympathizers. (*Right*) A suspect is held prisoner in one of the many **concentration camps** (*above*).

(*Above*) **Max Morlock** (second from right), the West German inside-right, scores against Hungary in the soccer World Cup Final at Berne, Switzerland on July 4, 1954. West Germany won 3–2 to take the Jules Rimet Trophy. (*Left*) On a wind-swept track at Iffley Road, Oxford, **Roger Bannister** completes the first under Four-Minute Mile, May 6, 1954. His time was three minutes, 59 seconds.

New life had already been pumped into the House Un-American Activities Committee by **Senator Joseph McCarthy** when he had purged Hollywood of "The Red Menace". In 1954, he took on the Army and the case of Private David Schine, a close friend of McCarthy's lawyer Roy M Cohn. The result was disastrous for McCarthy, for among others he had infuriated Eisenhower himself.

Track 17

(*Above*) **Sophia Loren** is surprised that she should be the subject of photographic attention at the awards ceremony in Rome where **Marlon Brando** (on right) received the Francesco Pasinetti Prize for his role in *On the Waterfront*. (*Right*) **Maria Callas** takes a celebrity dinner in her stride at the Chicago Hilton following her performance in Bellini's *Norma* at the Lyric Theater of Chicago, November 1954.

One of the most striking and original films of 1954 was Federico Fellini's **La Strada**, the story of a half-witted peasant girl sold to a circus strong man. (*Above*) Giulietta Masina and Anthony Quinn in a still from the film.

(*Above*) While Eva Marie Saint looks on, Karl Malden (on left) comforts Marlon Brando (center) in the final sequence of Kazan's **On the Waterfront**. The film won Oscars for Budd Schulberg's great script, Kazan, Brando, Saint, and Boris Kaufman's photography.

The playwright Arthur Miller first met Marilyn Monroe (*below and right*, in portraits by Baron) at a Hollywood party. During the evening, the actress Evelyn Keyes said to Miller: "They'll eat her alive". They did, though it took 12 years before Hollywood, politicians, and the media finally had their fill. Miller, Monroe's third husband, and a man who knew her better than anyone, described her as "ludicrously provocative", with a "perfection that aroused a wish to defend it... though I suspected how tough she must be to have survived so long". She was, briefly, the icon of an industry, a culture, a nation, and a planet.

Two well-stacked bodies. (*Above*) Monroe and her second husband, the baseball star Joe DiMaggio, step out following their wedding in January 1954. (*Right*) On a USO tour during the Korean War, Monroe faces a hillside covered in ravenous servicemen, while signing a fistful of autographs.

Marilyn Monroe

(*Left*) Perhaps the most famous movie still of all time. Marilyn Monroe stands on the subway ventilation grating in Billy Wilder's *The Seven Year Itch*. (*Above*) Monroe, in the same dress and on the set with Wilder. (*Right*) An authorized studio portrait of 1955.

1955 **Marilyn Monroe**

In January 1955, Communist forces on the Chinese mainland began to threaten Nationalist Chinese settlements on the **Tachen Islands**, some 200 miles (320 kilometers) north of Formosa (now Taiwan). The US Navy evacuated some 14,000 civilians from the Islands (*left*), and talks were held by the United States and General Chiang Kai-Shek, leader of Nationalist China. (*Above*) Chiang Kai-Shek meets Secretary of State John Foster Dulles, March 5, 1955.

On February 28, 1955, Israeli forces
attacked Egyptian army posts on the Gaza
Strip, killing 36 men. Arab leaders
protested. Fearing war, members of the
Arab League met in Cairo (*above*). Both
talks and fighting continued for six months.

(*Above*) This photograph issued by the Israeli Government Press Office in October 1955 shows a young **Ariel Sharon** (second from left) when a paratroop officer, with General **Moshe Dayan** on his immediate left. It was taken just after Israeli and Egyptian forces clashed in Sinai.

Marlon Brando received his Oscar for
On the Waterfront in March 1955, when
it was comically presented to him at the
Academy Awards by Bob Hope (*above*).
With his customary modesty, the pianist
and showman **Liberace** poses by his
back-garden pool in Hollywood (*right*).

🔘 *Track 19*

The defeat of the French in 1954 had done little to stabilize the region of **Vietnam**. In the south there was division between the US-backed President Ngo Dinh Diem and the formerly French backed anti-Communist Binh Xuyen faction. (*Above*) Diem at an agricultural show in 1955, minutes before an attempt on his life. (*Right*) Women and children flee fighting on the streets between the two factions, May 1955.

135

1955

The Paris Treaties came into effect on May 5, 1955, granting West Germany full sovereignty under the leadership of **Konrad Adenauer**. (*Right*) *Time* magazine correspondent James Bell keeps an eye on Adenauer as the Chancellor departs in a car, September 1955. (*Left*) Delegates at the **Paris Conference**: (left to right) Pierre Mendès-France, Adenauer, Anthony Eden, and John Foster Dulles.

On June 11, 1955, Pierre Levegh was driving a Mercedes in the **Le Mans** 24-hour Formula 1 race when the car ahead of him suddenly braked. Levegh's car hit the tail ramp of the car ahead and catapulted into the crowd, killing 80 people and injuring more than 100 others. (*Above*) Levegh rounds a bend just before the crash. (*Left*) The aftermath of the crash. Parts of Levegh's car were made of magnesium, which caused intense fires.

🔊 *Track 20*

On July 15, 1955 the world's greatest amusement park opened in Anaheim, California. **Disneyland** was an immediate success, a mixture of fantasy and adventure in true Hollywood style. (*Above*) Walt Disney, part cowboy, part uncle, and all business-man. (*Right*) Children burst through the entrance to Sleeping Beauty's castle.

 Track 21

The grief that love can bring... (*Above*) In England **Princess Margaret** returns to her home in Clarence House after a weekend with the man she loved, Group Captain Peter Townsend, October 17, 1955. Two weeks later, Buckingham Palace announced that Margaret and Townsend would not marry. The demands of royalty overcame the yearnings of the heart.

Ruth Ellis was a British club manager and model who shot and killed her lover, David Blakely, on April 10, 1955. It took the jury at her trial just 14 minutes to find her guilty of murder, and on July 13 she was hanged at Holloway Prison. (*Above*) Ruth Ellis in the flat above her club on the Brompton Road, Knightsbridge, London.

(*Right*) In October leaders of the **Big Four**—France, Britain, the United States, and the USSR—met at Geneva to discuss German re-unification, and the future of NATO and the Warsaw Pact. (*Above*—left to right) Bulganin, Eisenhower, Eden, and Faure. (*Below*—left to right) Mrs Dwight Eisenhower, Mrs Anthony Eden, and Mme Edgar Faure, as society would then have labeled them.

(*Above*) **Habib Bourguiba** (in fez) returns in triumph to Tunisia after three years exile in France, June 3, 1955. Bourguiba was then leader of the New-Destour Nationalist Party and would shortly become President of Tunisia. He was in office for only two years, but brought independence to his country.

After several months of political instability in Morocco, the French decided to re-instate the former Sultan Sidi **Mohammad ben Yussef**. (*Above*) Jubilant supporters of Mohammad ben Yussef celebrate his return in the countryside outside Casablanca, September 12, 1955.

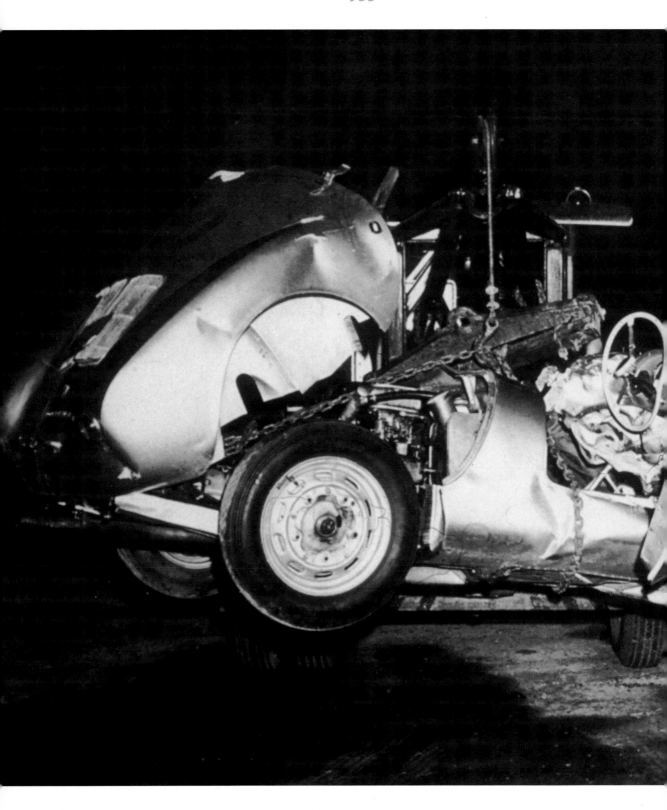

In May 1955 the movie star **James Dean** (*above*) traded in his Porsche 356 Speedster for the more powerful 550 Spyder. He then hired George Barris, later to design the *Batmobile*, to customize the Spyder, but Warner Brothers barred Dean from racing while he was filming *Giant*. On September 30, Dean was killed at the wheel of what his language coach had dubbed "Little Bastard" (*left*).

🔘 *Track 23*

In the 1950s, London's **smog** was infamous. A vitriolic mixture of mist or fog, smoke from open fires, and the increasing amounts of car exhaust, smog seared into the lungs, killing thousands each winter. (*Left*) A London Transport employee guides a bus through the streets with a flaming torch. (*Above*) A couple improvise masks in a London park.

"The movement gathers momentum..."—Martin Luther King Jnr. In the wake of the refusal by Rosa Parks to give up her seat on a bus to a white man, black citizens of **Montgomery** walk to work as part of their boycott of the bus system, February 1956. Another nine months were to pass before segregation on Alabama buses was declared illegal, and yet another month before the new law came into effect.

🔊 *Track 24*

The decision in the case of *Brown et al v the Board of Education of Topeka et al* (1954) is at last put into effect. National Guardsmen stand watch as students leave a school bus as racial **de-segregration** is forced through at the beginning of the school year, September 1956.

In dozens of images in the TV section of a store, **Dwight D Eisenhower** explains to Americans why he has decided to run for president a second time, March 1956. Eisenhower was an accomplished TV performer and election campaigner. The campaign slogan "I Like Ike" convinced enough voters to give him a landslide victory in November.

The epitome of happy motoring in the mid-1950s. A regally dressed model poses by a chrome-festooned Pontiac La Parisienne in a shallow pool at the **New York Coliseum Auto Show**, December 7, 1956.

Track 25

The **Bedouin B collapsible trailer caravan** was "designed for comfort", though a misty English morning in November may not have been the best time to put it on display. It converted from trailer to "spacious home" in four minutes flat.

Seventy-five-year-old **Pablo Picasso**
mixes his palette for the camera
during the filming of the documentary
The Mystery of Picasso in 1956.
He was still living in France, and still
bitterly opposed to the rule of
General Franco in his native Spain.

Irish playwright and author **Brendan Behan** in full flow at the Fitzroy Tavern, London, June 30, 1956. Behan was then living in London though still bitterly opposed to the way British governments had treated his fellow Irish men and women.

Marilyn Monroe and **Arthur Miller** head off in a Ford Thunderbird for their honeymoon in Connecticut, July 1956. Monroe had just finished filming *The Prince and the Showgirl*; Miller had just faced the last of his hearings before the HUAC. Happy days lay ahead, though Miller later wrote of Monroe that "with all her radiance she was surrounded by darkness".

The Prince and the Showgirl—the moment when Monseigneur Gilles Barthe bestowed nuptial benediction to **Rainier** Louis Henri Maxence Bertrand de Grimaldi, Prince of Monaco and **Grace Patricia Kelly**, at their wedding in St Nicholas Cathedral, Monte Carlo, April 1956.

🔘 *Track 26*

(*Right*) **Joan Collins** attends the European premiere of *The King and I* on September 12, 1956. It was a busy year for her. She made three films—*The Opposite Sex*, *Sea Wife and Biscuit*, and *Island in the Sun*, and divorced her first husband Maxwell Reed after extraordinary rumors that he had attempted to sell her to an Arabian sheikh.

🔘 *Track 27*

(*Above*) **Brigitte Bardot** takes a break from filming Roger Vadim's "*... And God Created Woman*" in St Tropez, for a quick cigarette and a glance at a recent magazine article on herself. The film was described by the *Catholic League of Decency* as "an open violation of conventional morality".

While Charlton Heston, on screen as Moses in *The Ten Commandments*, parts the waters, the occupants of numerous gas-guzzling Buicks, Oldsmobiles, and Mercurys sip their Cokes, munch their popcorn and, in some cases, get down to a little petting at the **Drive-In**.

(*Left*) The front of the **Cameo Cinema, London** on June 12, 1956. The film on show was *The Flesh is Weak*, a tale of a young girl from Reading, England, lured into prostitution. It was a film sold to the public as essential viewing if they wished to prevent their daughters suffering such a fate.

(*Above*) The front of the **Paramount Theater, New York City** on the night Alan Freed's show hit town. Freed was a disc-jockey who quickly assumed the title "King of Rock 'n' Roll" and said "There's nothing critics can do to stop this new solid beat of American music from sweeping across the land in a tidal wave of happiness." It made him very rich.

"Hep" places to meet and greet in. (*Above*) A customer sips espresso delight in one of London's new **coffee bars** of the 1950s. (*Left*) **Teddy Boys** in their neo-Edwardian finery play the slot machines on Canvey Island. (*Right*) **Rock 'n' Roll** night at the Royal Dance Hall, Tottenham, London.

🔊 *Track 28*

(*Above*) The young Elvis attends to his hair as manager **Colonel Tom Parker** (left) discusses terms with **Ed Sullivan** (right). It was Elvis's second appearance on the *Ed Sullivan Show*, October 28, 1956.

🔘 *Track 29*

(*Left*) **Elvis** live at the Olympia Theater, Miami, Florida on August 14, 1956. The mother of one of Elvis's young fans said: "I just came because the kids wanted to. I was curious. Now I know. Look at him. He looks like a hound dog in heat and sounds like a sick cat."

There had been other challenges to Soviet domination. In 1953 Polish Catholics had protested against the confinement of Cardinal Wyszynski, and violent demonstrations occurred in East Germany. Hungary was different. On October 23, 1956 students in Budapest challenged the Stalinist First Secretary Matyas Rakosi. The State Secret Police (the AVH) fired on the students and the people rose in fury.

Moscow forced Rakosi to resign, but there was to be no compromise. Early in November, Soviet tanks rumbled into Hungary. Bitter fighting broke out. Over the next four weeks 10,000 people died in Budapest alone. Without intervention by the West, however, the rising was doomed, and the West was not prepared to risk the possibility of all-out war with the Soviet Union. The end came late in November with one last desperate radio message: "We don't have much time... Help the Hungarian nation, help its workers, its peasants, and its intellectuals... Help! Help! Help!..."

(*Right*) Daniel Sego (third from left) stands over the remains of a mammoth statue of Joseph Stalin. It was Sego who had cut off the head from the rest of the statue.

(*Left*) On an upper floor of a Budapest apartment block, Hungarian freedom fighters lie in wait for the approach of the Soviet invaders, November 1956.

October 31, 1956. Trial and sentence (from left to right): a group of AVH members face their accusers on the streets of Budapest; their plea for mercy has failed; the execution begins; justice of a kind has been implemented, though the men were young and may well have joined the AVH for economic rather than ideological reasons; a freedom fighter administers the *coup de grace* to the sole survivor of the first killing.

The Hungarian Uprising   1956

(*Left*) An elderly citizen of Budapest weeps as she watches Soviet tanks and troops in action against the anti-Communist uprising, November 12, 1956.

(*Below*) An officer in the Red Army draws his pistol as he advances on *Picture Post* photographer Jack Esten, Budapest, November 12. The Soviet authorities were determined that as little information as possible on events in Hungary should reach the outside world.

The Hungarian Uprising   1956

(*Above*) Russian tanks on the streets of
Budapest, November 1956. Images like this
shook the Western world, but the Hungarians
were still left without any help.

In October 1956, French, British, and Israeli troops attacked Egypt following the nationalization by Egypt of the **Suez Canal**. (*Left*) A crowd gathers at the statue of Ferdinand de Lesseps, creator of the Suez Canal, in Port Said. Departing French troops have left a *tricolore* in de Lesseps' outstretched hand. (*Above*) A convoy trapped in the Suez Canal during the crisis of 1956 awaits the canal's re-opening.

After a brief spell of fighting, the UN
and the United States put pressure on the
French and British to withdraw. (*Above*)
UN troops follow the departing British
through **Port Said**, while Egyptians shout
"Nasser for ever!", November 24, 1956.

(*Above*) Egyptian President, **Gamal Abdul Nasser**, the man whose nationalization of the Suez Canal incensed the British government of Sir Anthony Eden and thereby provoked the British invasion. Nasser's ultimate success hastened the end of the British Empire.

Militarily, the invasion of the Canal Zone had been a great success. Politically, it was a disaster, splitting both France and Britain into those who supported the action and those who were passionately against it. (*Above*) British soldiers wave to **UN peacekeeping troops** as Britain withdraws from Suez, December 2, 1956.

(*Right*) Arab civilians pick their way through the **rubble** of the streets following air raids and shelling from British forces. Whole villages were destroyed following the invasion, though the actual fighting had lasted less than two weeks.

The port of **Aden**, on the tip of the Arabian peninsula where the Red Sea and the Gulf of Aden converge, had long been a refueling station for the ships that patrolled Britain's eastern empire. That Empire was fast crumbling, but Aden remained strategically important in the movement of oil from the Middle East to the West. (*Left*) The BP crude oil distillation unit at Aden.

In 1957 Little Aden, as it was known, came under attack by Yemeni forces, seeking to end British presence there. (*Above*) An RAF officer in discussion with local troops. The fighting was to continue sporadically until the British finally withdrew in 1964.

After two years of negotiations, the **Treaty of Rome**, which established the European Economic Community, was finally signed on March 25, 1957. The signatories were France, West Germany, Italy, Belgium, the Netherlands, and Luxembourg. (*Above*) Delegates sign the Treaty in the Campadoglio, Rome. Two months later, at a meeting of **NATO** officials in Bonn, (*right*), the Secretary of State John Foster Dulles announced that the United States would keep its troops in Western Europe.

In March 1957 the old West African colony known as the Gold Coast achieved independence under its new name of Ghana. (*Left*) A quartet of Ghanaian politicians at the Independence ceremonies, (left to right): A Caseley Hayford, Komla Agbeli Gbedemah, **Kwame Nkrumah,** and Kojo Botsio. Nkrumah became the first Prime Minister of the new state, popular with both the outgoing British and his own people. (*Above*) The parade to celebrate **Ghana's independence**, Accra, March 6, 1957.

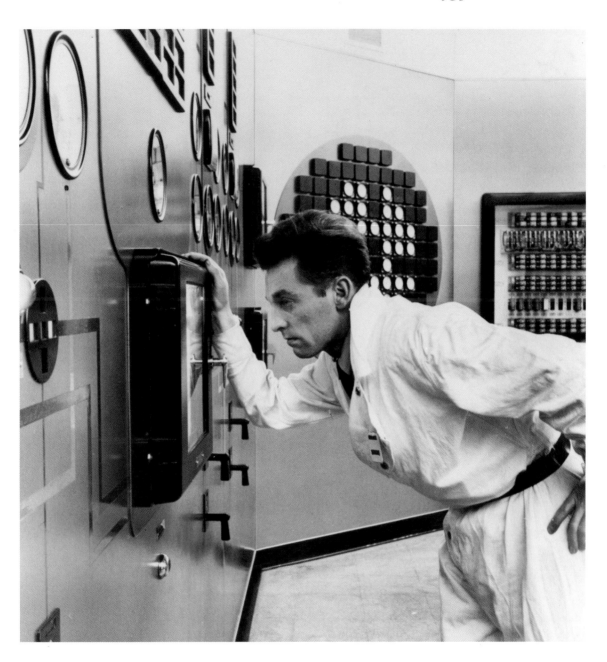

Track 32

The 1950s built on the scientific and technological progress pioneered in World War II. (*Left*) The giant 250-feet (80-meter) diameter Radio Telescope at **Jodrell Bank**, Cheshire. (*Above*) Monitoring the performance of Britain's first nuclear power station at Calder Hall in **Windscale**, Cumberland, February 25, 1957. Within a few years, the United States and several European countries were using nuclear energy.

On September 3, 1957, black students were refused entry to the Central High School in **Little Rock**, Arkansas. (*Above*) National Guardsmen, under orders from Governor Orval Faubus, look on as Elizabeth Eckford (on left) is pursued by white parents.

Three weeks later, President Eisenhower ordered Federal troops to Little Rock to ensure that **de-segregation** of the school was implemented. (*Above*) Federal troops face down jeering white racists.

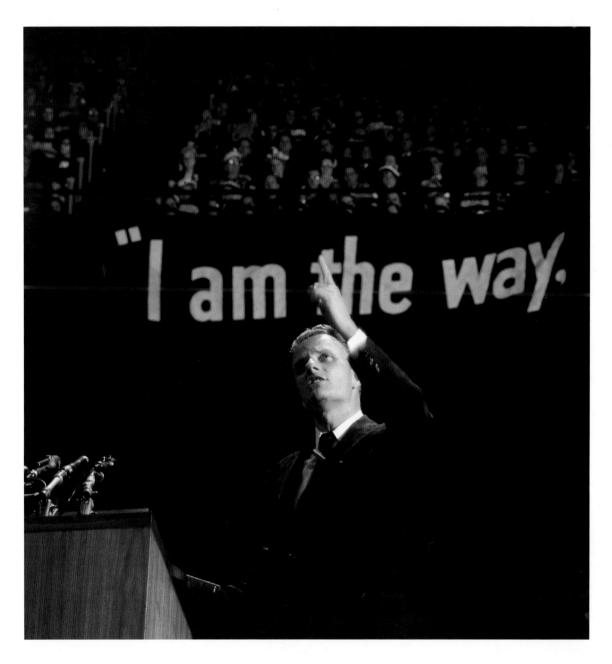

Track 33

As prosperity increased during the 1950s, crowds flocked to cinemas, concert halls, and theaters. (*Left*) **Laurence Olivier** struts his way across stage as Archie Rice in a rehearsal of John Osborne's *The Entertainer*, April 10, 1957. (*Above*) One hundred thousand others flocked to Madison Square Garden to hear the evangelist **Billy Graham** preach the Word of God.

For the increasingly affluent young generation, there were "kicks" to be found in a variety of locations. (*Above*) A couple sip their Pepsis in **Butlin's Ocean Hotel**, Saltdean, England. The box camera on the table is there to record some of the highlights of their honeymoon.

A revival of traditional New Orleans jazz swept much of Europe in the later 1950s, and the songs of Buddy Bolden, Jelly Roll Morton, and W C Handy were heard wherever the fans gathered. (*Above*) A **riverboat shuffle** on a ferry bound for Calais, France, June 3, 1957. Note the tea chest double bass.

The birth of the LP led to a boom in the sale of recorded classical music, which in turn boosted attendances at live concerts. (*Above*) The conductor **Wolfgang Sawallisch** at a Bayreuth Festival rehearsal. (*Left*) Erich Auerbach's photo of the French cellist **Pierre Fournier**. (*Right*) The German composer **Paul Hindemith** at a press conference in Munich, August 7, 1957.

Haute Couture confidently paraded its wares on street, catwalk, and the pages of glossy magazines. (*Above*) Model Bronwen Pugh, later to be Lady Astor, wears a "little black number" on a Paris street. (*Left*) A gazelle mask by Aubry, designed for a Paris Shrove Tuesday Ball.

(*Left*) A model of the satellite *Sputnik I*, on show in the Soviet Pavilion at the Brussels World's Fair, April 1958. (*Right*) Dr Fred L Whipple (left) and Dr Josef A Hynek plot the orbit of *Sputnik I* from the Smithsonian Astrophysical Observatory, Harvard University, Cambridge, Massachusetts, October 1957.

It may not have been written in the stars, but there had been increasing certainty among scientists and engineers that space—"the final frontier"—would soon be accessible. That day came on October 4, 1957, with the launching of the world's first man-made satellite. East and West had engaged in expensive competition for the honor, but the USSR beat the United States by almost three months with *Sputnik I*. America's *Explorer I* satellite followed on February 1, 1958. What astonished US scientists—and clearly depressed Wernher von Braun (*right*), Director of the US Ballistic Missile Agency, was *Sputnik*'s weight—184 lb (83.5 kilos), eight times the weight of *Explorer*. The Soviet success served only to intensify the East/West rivalry for the next 12 years.

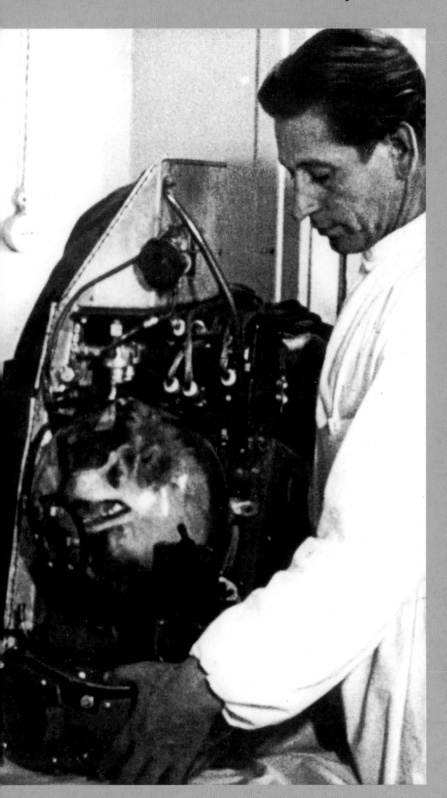

Within a month of *Sputnik I*'s pioneer voyage, the USSR launched *Sputnik II*, which carried Laika (*right*), a stray dog plucked from the streets of Moscow, as passenger. Laika became famous, a hero of the Soviet Union—there was even a cigarette named after her (*above*). The dog sadly did not survive the voyage, perishing when the specially built space capsule (*left*) burned up on re-entry to the earth's atmosphere.

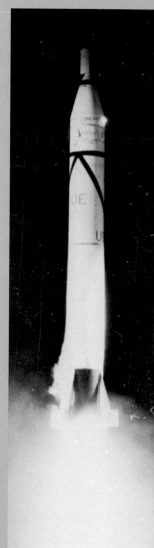

In happier mood, Wernher von Braun (*above*) poses with a somewhat primitive model of the US space satellite *Explorer I*. (*Right*) *Explorer* blasts off from Cape Canaveral, Florida, February 1, 1958. The following month, however, von Braun announced that US space research was "several years" behind that of the USSR.

The Space Race   1958

In the summer of 1958, the United States embarked on a series of lunar probes from Cape Canaveral. The first launch (*above*) took place in August but exploded 77 seconds after lift off. In January 1959 *Lunik 1* missed the Moon by 6,000 miles (9,655 kilometers), but in September *Lunik 2* was smack on target.

On February 7, 1958, Matt Busby, **Manchester United** manager, briefed his team (*left*) before their European Cup soccer match with Red Star. Hours later, (*above*) the plane carrying the team home crashed at **Munich Airport**. (*Right*) Bobby Charlton recovers in a Munich hospital. Eight England footballers and 13 other passengers were killed.

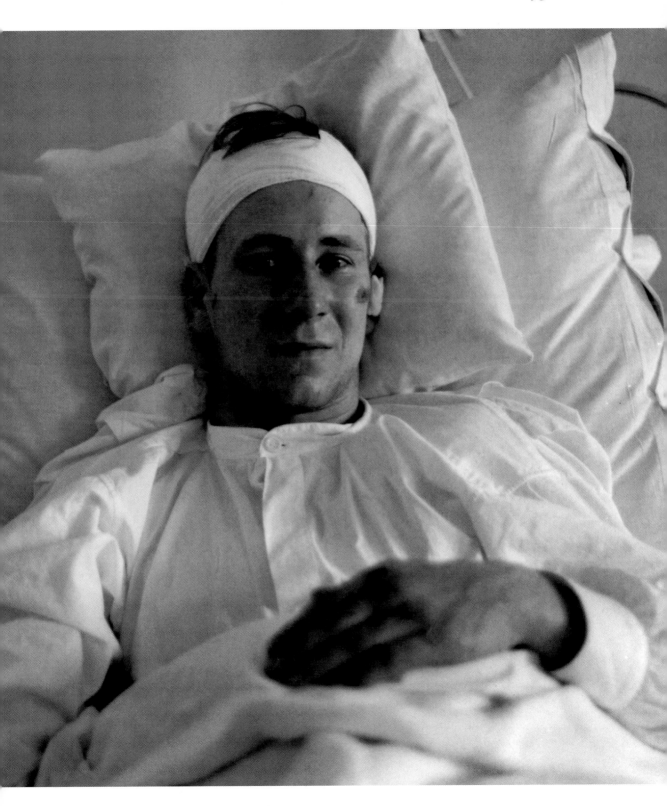

In March 1958, the Army drafted **Elvis Presley**. (*Right*) Presley takes the lead at the induction center and is sworn in. (*Far right*) Private Presley marches to barracks at Fort Chaffee Reception Center. (*Above*) In his Number One uniform, Elvis contemplates the years ahead. He spent more time with his guitar than with a gun.

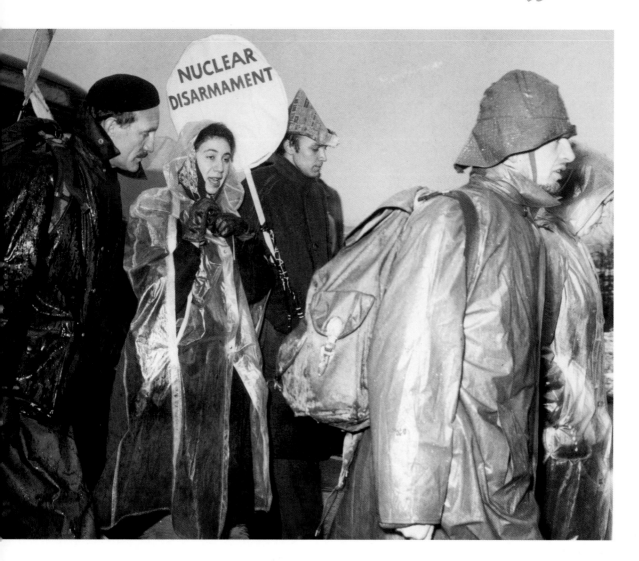

The new pressure group—the **Campaign for Nuclear Disarmament**—was established in February 1958. Two months later, CND organized the first March from London to the Atomic Weapons Research establishment at Aldermaston. (*Right*) Demonstrators set out along almost traffic-free streets, April 4, 1958. (*Above*) Three days later, the rain-soaked marchers reach Aldermaston.

MARCH FROM
LONDON
☮ TO ☮
ALDERMASTON

🔵 *Track 36*

Expo '58, the Brussels World's fair, opened on April 17, 1958. It was the first World's Fair to be held since World War II, and had taken three years to construct. More than 42 million visitors came, many specifically to see the Atomium (*left*), a giant model of an iron crystal, each sphere representing an atom. Soviet exhibits (*above*) included a model space satellite, and the inevitable statue of Lenin.

CIRCULATION ROUTIERE

In May 1958, General Jacques **Massu** (*right*) led a revolt of French Army officers and settlers in **Algeria**. Their fears were that the French Government would give in to the demands of native Algerians for independence. (*left*) French Military Police attempt to keep order on the streets of Algiers during Massu's revolt. The General lived on until 2002.

One month after the Algerian revolt, the French Government capitulated and gave **General de Gaulle** (*left*) the "exceptional" powers that he had demanded to lead France. (*Right*) De Gaulle visits Algiers. The *pieds noirs* were delighted to see him, but came to regard him as a traitor when he agreed to Algerian independence.

The **1958 FIFA World Cup** was a triumph for Brazil, who beat Sweden 5–2 in the soccer Final at Stockholm, June 29, 1958. (*Left*) Edson Arantes do Nascimento, better known as **Pelé**, challenges the Swedish goalkeeper Kalle Svensson in the penalty area. (*Above*) The victorious Brazilian team carry Swedish flags on their lap of honor after the match.

On August 24, 1958, five black men
were attacked by a mob of white youths
in the **Notting Hill** area of London. Six
nights later, some 200 blacks and
whites fought a running battle on the
streets. (*Above*) A police sergeant
confronts a black citizen in Notting Hill.

The violence escalated. On the night of August 31, there were 400 rioters in Notting Hill. The following night, up to 2,000 white men, women, and youths were attacking areas whose inhabitants were predominately black. (*Above*) **Four youths** remanded at West London Police Court following the riots.

On October 9, 1958, **Pope Pius XII** died in Rome. He had
been Pontiff since March 1939, and, though he had attracted
criticism for his pro-Nazi leanings, was regarded by many
as a saint. (*Above*) Crowds surge to see the body of Pius at
the Castel Gandolfo. The newly elected Pope was **John XXIII**,
a heartier and more outgoing "Papa" than the ascetic Pius.
(*Right*) The new Pope is kissed by an inmate at the Regina
Coeli Prison in Rome, December 27, 1958.

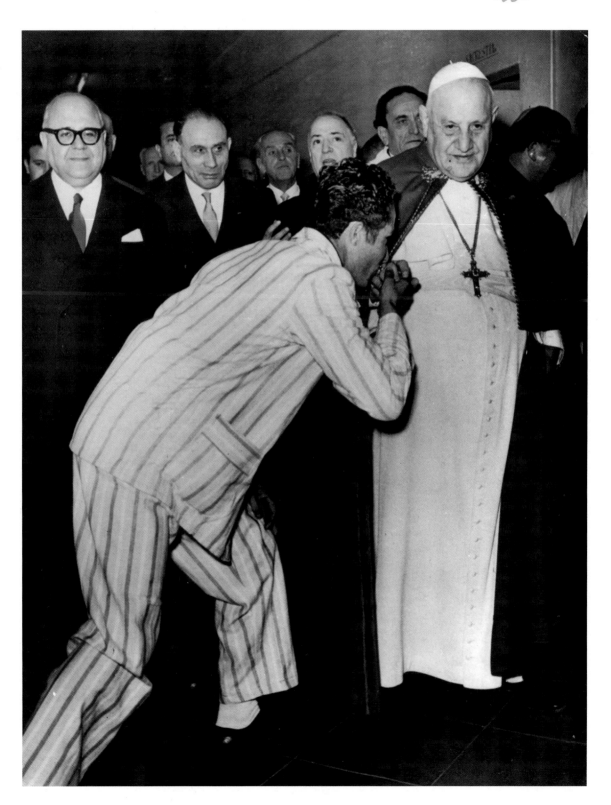

Although not the first
commercial passenger jet
airliner, the **Boeing 707** made
history on October 26, 1958
when Pan-Am inaugurated the
first trans-Atlantic service
between New York and Paris.
It was a close call. The 707's
range capability barely
extended from America to
Europe. (*Left*) A 707 in flight.

🔘 *Track 37*

The grandeur of **automobile design** cruised on throughout the 1950s. Sales steadily rose, gasoline was as cheap as it would ever be, and there were happy faces in the boardrooms of Detroit. (*Above*) An auto-pilot speed-regulating device is fastened to the wheel of a 1958 Chrysler.

🔘 *Track 38*

One half of the American Dream... the neat house and the freckled children are missing, but the good-looking couple and the "groovy wheels" are right there. Model man and woman pose for a promotional shot beside a **Chevrolet XP-700 Corvette**, one of the smartest cars of 1958.

(*Above*) Part of the retrospective exhibition of the art of **Jean Arp** at the Museum of Modern Art, New York, October 1958.
(*Right*) Park Avenue Towers: The Seagram Building, designed by **Ludwig Mies van der Rohe**, and Lever House (on right).

After five years of struggle to overthrow the corrupt government of Fulgencio Batista, the Cuban Revolution gained momentum in 1958. Marxist guerrillas led by Fidel and Raul Castro, Che Guevara, Camilo Cienfuegos, and Jaime Vega moved from their hideouts in the Sierra Maestra mountains to attack major cities. On December 31, Santa Clara fell to the guerrillas, and Batista fled from Cuba the following day. On January 2, 1959, Castro's forces took Santiago de Cuba while Guevara and Cienfuegos entered Havana. With triumph came retribution. Church property was confiscated, and hundreds of Batista's men were publicly tried for human rights abuses and war crimes. From being the playground of the rich, Cuba became, almost overnight, a dangerous outpost of Communism in the eyes of the West.

On the road to Havana. (*Above*) Members of the 26th July Militia break from their march to listen to one of Fidel Castro's victory addresses. (*Right*) Castro (in glasses, with cigar) brings news of the Revolution's success on his journey from the Sierra Maestra to Havana, January 5, 1959.

In its later stages, as success seemed assured, the Revolution was well recorded by the camera. Images of its charismatic leaders and its almost atavistic warriors were flashed around the world. (*Above*) Camilo Cienfuegos (center) enters Havana. (*Left*) Che Guevara, January 7, 1959. (*Right*) Raul Castro at a victory celebration some months later. (*Far right*) Fidel Castro with yet another cigar and another hero's welcome.

(*Above*) From the top of the Hilton Hotel, Fidel Castro (on right) and friends gaze out across the city of Havana, and perhaps plan a new future for the clubs, casinos and *bordellos* that flourished under Batista. (*Right*) Cubans greet the dawn of the new era, January 1959. (*Left*) On July 26, 1959, six years after the Revolution began at the Moncada Barracks, Castro addresses a vast crowd in Havana.

s the Scotch

2ᴬ

One by one the flag was lowered and the trumpets
silenced in the old British Empire. On March 1, 1959, the
Greek nationalist leader Archbishop **Makarios** returned
to Cyprus after three years of exile in Britain. **Enosis**—
complete union with Greece—was ruled out, but an
agreement was signed for joint Greek and Turkish rule.
(*Left*) Makarios in London, February 1959. (*Above*) Crowds
in Cyprus welcome the return of Makarios, March 4, 1959.

White rule survived in **Rhodesia** until the end of the 1970s, but not without problems. In 1959, with support from the ANC, widespread riots broke out in Northern Rhodesia following the arrest of Dr Hastings Banda. (*Left*) Armed African workers on the **Kariba Dam** project go on strike. (*Above*) Members of the Rhodesian armed forces on guard during the strike and disturbances, February 1959.

(Left) **A young Hawaiian** holds a flag confirming the good news. Though opposition to statehood came from plantation owners in Hawaii and Southerners in Congress who disliked the mixed race element in Hawaii's population, President Eisenhower welcomed Hawaii, wishing the new state "prosperity, security and happiness".

(Above) **Hawaiians** take to the streets to celebrate their admission to the United States of America, August 21, 1959. In a referendum two months earlier, the people of Hawaii had voted 17 to 1 in favor of becoming the 50th State of the Union.

The "**Kitchen Debate**" between Soviet Premier Nikita Krushchev and visiting Vice-President Richard Nixon took place in the model kitchen at the American National Exhibition in Moscow, July 1959. Krushchev was appalled at the gadgetry on show, asking if there was a machine that "puts food into the mouth and pushes it down". Nixon backed a non-military technological contest, saying "with modern weapons it doesn't make any difference if war comes. We both have had it".

🔘 *Track 40*

WITNESS

In media terms, "the spit hit the fan" twice in 1959. The radio career of DJ Alan Freed (*right*) was wrecked by **"payola"**, the payment of money to DJs to plug certain records. **Charles Van Doren** won $138,000 in a TV quiz show called *Twenty One*, having been fed the answers and coached in how to perform by programme officials. (*Left*) Van Doren testifies before the House Committee on Interstate and Foreign Commerce.

The blockbuster movie of 1959 was MGM's **Ben Hur** which won six Oscars, including that of Best Picture and Best Director (William Wyler). (*Right*) Charlton Heston in whip-lashing mode as Ben Hur. (*Left*) Sammy Davis Junior as Sportin' Life in the Samuel Goldwyn movie production of George Gershwin's **Porgy and Bess**.

C/724-20

The Tale of the Sparkly Dress… (*Left*) Part 1: Fifty-three-year-old **Josephine Baker** gives it all she's got at the Olympia, Paris, March 1959. (*Right*) Part 2: Twenty-two-year-old **Shirley Bassey** at a cabaret performance. It was the year of her hit *As Long As He Needs Me*, from Lionel Bart's *Oliver!*

A wide-angle lens' view of the **Solomon R Guggenheim Museum**, New York City. Its designer, Frank Lloyd Wright, who died on April 9, 1959, wrote of it: "Here is the ideal I propose for the architecture of the machine age... for how an ideal American architecture should develop..."

🔘 Track 41

The exploration of space continued with some more willing than others to take part. (*Right*) Project Mercury astronaut **Donald Slayton** rides an orbital attitude simulator at Langley Air Force base, Virginia. Due to an erratic heart condition, he was the only member of the seven man crew not to fly on the mission in 1962. (*Left*) **Sam the Rhesus monkey** after his return to earth, December 10, 1959.

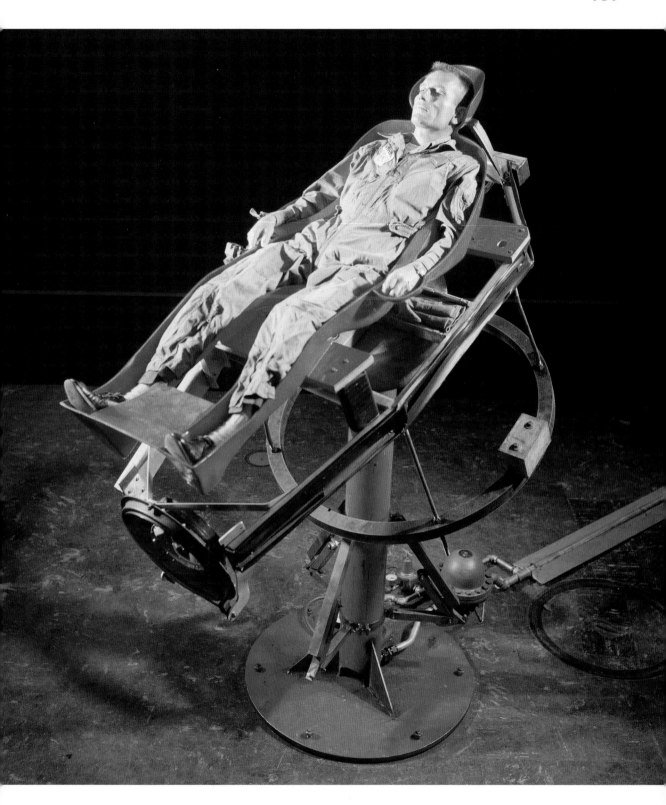

Index